Original title:
Autumn's Whispered Words

Copyright © 2024 Creative Arts Management OÜ
All rights reserved.

Author: Clement Portlander
ISBN HARDBACK: 978-9916-85-752-6
ISBN PAPERBACK: 978-9916-85-753-3

A Canvas Painted in Twilight

In hues of purple, gold, and blue,
Each stroke a memory, a dream in view.
The sun dips low, embracing the night,
A canvas transformed by fading light.

Shadows dance on the whispering ground,
As day bows out, a new hush is found.
Colors merge in the softest sigh,
A masterpiece crafted as day says goodbye.

Whispers Among the Withering

In gardens where the silence clings tight,
Leaves flutter softly, fading from sight.
Once vibrant, now gray under time's stern hand,
Each rustle a tale from a forgotten land.

Withering blooms, their secrets unfold,
In the whispers of dusk, they silently hold.
Life's fleeting moments, like petals, will wane,
Yet beauty resides in the echoes of pain.

The Confluence of Time and Leaves

Time trickles down like the stream of a brook,
Softly cradled in the nooks of a book.
Leaves gather stories upon each winding path,
The dance of their fall speaks of nature's wrath.

In the confluence where minutes collide,
Memories linger, like shadows they bide.
Seasons entwined in a graceful embrace,
Each leaf a chapter, each moment a trace.

Secrets in the Smoky Air

In the twilight's haze, secrets swirl around,
Carried on whispers, like smoke from the ground.

Cherished confessions, like embers that glow,
Unraveling stories that no one will know.

The night holds its breath, shrouded in mist,
An echoing silence that begs to be kissed.
In the embrace of the dark, mysteries laid bare,
Life lingers softly in the smoky air.

Whispering Pines and Distant Hues

In the forest deep where shadows play,
Whispering pines sing secrets of the day.
Their needles dance with the soft sigh of air,
Distant hues of twilight, a painter's affair.

Sunset drapes golden on trunks so tall,
Each whispering breath, nature's gentle call.
The world melts away in a palette divine,
Among the whispering pines, I feel so fine.

Conversations with the Wandering Wind

Beneath the vast sky, I hear the wind speak,
Carrying tales from mountains unique.
It twirls through the trees, a dancer so free,
In conversations wild, it calls out to me.

With every soft gust, it brings laughter and tears,
Whispers of ages, of hopes and of fears.
Through valleys and canyons, the stories it spins,

In the dance of the breezes, my spirit begins.

Reflections on a Dimming Horizon

As daylight fades into hues of regret,
The horizon glows with a soft silhouette.
Rippling waters catch the last of the sun,
In reflections of moments, both lost and won.

Embers of twilight, like memories blend,
Each shadow a whisper, each change an end.
Yet in the dimming light, hope flickers anew,
In the canvas of night, possibilities brew.

Colors that Recall Forgotten Dreams

In a palette of dusk, forgotten dreams bloom,
Brushstrokes of longing dispel every gloom.
Whispers of color in strokes bold and bright,
Bring forth the magic that sleeps in the night.

Each hue tells a story, a passion, a spark,
In the silence of memory, visions embark.
With laughter and sorrow, they dance and they swirl,
In colors that recall, a forgotten world.

Harvest Moon

In fields aglow with amber light,
The harvest moon begins its flight,
It spills its gold on ripened grain,
A bounteous gift from autumn's reign.

With whispers soft, the night unfolds,
As shadows dance and stories told,
The earth rejoices, spirits high,
Underneath the vast, embracing sky.

Twilight's Kiss

The day retreats with gentle grace,
As twilight paints the evening's face,
With hues of purple, gold, and rose,
A fleeting moment, time bestows.

Soft breezes carry secrets near,
In twilight's arms, our dreams appear,
The stars emerge, in silence weave,
A tapestry of night, we believe.

The Gathering of Windswept Tales

Among the trees, a story sways,
As autumn breathes in golden rays,
The leaves converse in rustling sound,
In whispered wisdom, magic found.

Each gust a verse, a memory spun,
Of laughter shared, of battles won,
They dance along the forest floor,
A gathering of tales, forevermore.

Echoes of a Parting Sun

As daylight fades and shadows grow,
The sun departs with lingering glow,
Its warmth embraced in twilight's sigh,
A tender farewell to the sky.

The world transforms with night's descent,
While echoes of the sun are lent,
In every heart, a spark remains,
A promise of return, through sun and rains.

Shadows of Orchard's Farewell

In twilight's brush, the orchard sighs,
As golden fruit bids soft goodbye,
Beneath the boughs, shadows dance,
Embracing dusk in tender glance.

The whispers of the breeze now slow,
Where vibrant hues begin to glow,
Each leaf a tale, each branch a dream,
In twilight's hold, the shadows gleam.

In the Quietude of Fall

The world exhales, the air is still,
Beneath the trees, the leaves fulfill,
A gentle rustle, nature's rhyme,
In autumn's hush, we find our time.

Golden harvests, pumpkin spice,
In quietude, there's sweet advice,
Embrace the change, let go of past,
In fall's embrace, the heart beats fast.

A Symphony of Crisp Leaves

Crisp leaves beneath our wandering feet,
A symphony in the air so sweet,
Rustling harmonies, a colorful show,
As breezes play where the soft winds blow.

Echoes of laughter, children at play,
In swirling gusts of a sunlit day,
Each vibrant tone, a note to sing,
In autumn's choir, we feel the spring.

The Lullaby of Harvest Moon

The moon ascends, a golden glow,
Illuminating fields below,
With gentle beams, it casts its light,
Embracing all in tranquil night.

The harvest sings a soft refrain,
Of fruits and grains that danced in rain,
While shadows weave their tender spell,
In nature's arms, all is well.

Whispers on the Wind

In twilight's hush, the secrets breathe,
Ghostly whispers dance through leaves,
Each sigh a story, spun and wreathed,
In nature's arms, the heart perceives.

Yet carried far, like dreams in flight,
The wind weaves tales of joys and fears,
Through branches bare and stars alight,
Echoes linger, soft as tears.

Beneath a Copper Canopy

Golden leaves on a winding track,
Cascades of amber swirl and fall,
Beneath the boughs that gently crack,
Nature's quilt wraps around us all.

The rustling whispers, a love song sweet,
Crickets play their evening tune,
With every step, the heart skips a beat,
In the embrace of autumn's boon.

The Language of Chill in the Air

As dusk descends, a breath of frost,
The world transforms, serene, withdrawn,
In every corner, warmth seems lost,
Yet stars awaken, heralding dawn.

Each shiver shared, the chill conspires,
To weave around us sparkling threads,
In whispers soft, the night inspires,
Our dreams ignited, while the daylight sheds.

Rumblings of the Coming Frost

In the quietude, a shiver stirs,
Winds gather strength, the air turns keen,
Nature's whisper, like distant purrs,
Promises of change in the dead of green.

Beneath the gaze of a silver moon,
The earth prepares for its deep retreat,
As shadows lengthen, a whispered tune,
Casts a spell where warmth and cold meet.

Tides of Turmeric and Tan

In fields where the golden spices grow,
The sun-kissed earth in a warm embrace flows,
Tides of turmeric dance beneath the skies,
As hues of saffron whisper soft goodbyes.

The breeze carries notes of summer's sweet song,

While shadows of twilight stretch long and strong,
In rituals of harvest, hands stained with gold,
Stories of the seasons are lovingly told.

When the World Slows Down

In the hush of twilight, time finds its pace,
The bustling thoughts begin to find their place,
Moments stretch like shadows on the ground,
When the chaos of life slips quietly around.

The stars appear like whispers in the dark,
Each one a promise, a mystical spark,
As silence settles, the heart learns to mend,
In the stillness, we find our journey's end.

The Embrace of Cool Nights

Cool nights wrap the world in a gentle sigh,
Moonlight drapes softly as the day says goodbye,

Stars twinkle in the fabric of the sky,
While under their watch, our dreams start to fly.

A breeze tells stories of ages long past,
Of lovers who lingered, their shadows cast,
In the embrace of night, quiet and deep,
The universe hums us into our sleep.

Conversations with the Setting Sun

Each dusk invites whispers from the horizon,
The sun dips low, painting skies that brighten,
With hues of coral and strokes of gold,
A canvas of silence, vast and bold.

As day surrenders to night's soft embrace,
I gather my thoughts in this sacred space,
In conversations with the fading light,
I find the peace that lingers after flight.

The Soft Murmur of Dusk

The sun dips low, a whisper in the sky,
Casting shadows where silent breezes sigh.
Crickets serenade the closing light,
As stars awaken, shimmering bright.

The horizon blushes in hues of deep red,
While twilight wraps the world in a soft thread.
Nightfall dances on the edge of dreams,
Where peace flows gently, in silver streams.

Twilight's Embrace in Rustling Foliage

In twilight's glow, the leaves softly sway,
A tender rustle, welcoming the day.
Branches beckon with secrets they keep,
As whispers of nature lull the world to sleep.

The air is thick with a fragrant repose,
As twilight beckons the night to propose.
A harmony woven in colors so bold,
Each leaf tells a story, waiting to unfold.

Nature's Golden Farewell

Golden rays scatter, a warm, soft embrace,
As day bids adieu, leaving naught but grace.
The sky ignites in a passionate dance,
A canvas of colors, nature's expanse.

With every sunset, the world breathes in deep,
A promise of dreams that the night will keep.
Nature sighs gently as darkness ascends,
In this fleeting moment, where beauty transcends.

The Rustle of Time's Tapestry

Threads of moments weave through the air,
A rustle of time that weaves memories rare.
Every heartbeat echoes, a story untold,
In the fabric of life where the past unfolds.

Each gust of wind carries whispers from yore,
Unraveling tales from the mountains to shore.
The tapestry stretches, with colors entwined,
A symphony crafted, forever aligned.

Murmurs in the Meadow

In golden fields where wildflowers sway,
The whispers of the breeze softly play,
Each blade of grass a story to unfold,
Painting memories in hues of gold.

Beneath the azure sky, a lullaby sings,
As butterflies dance on delicate wings,
Nature's gentle voice, a soothing embrace,
Where heartbeats align in tranquil space.

Fading Footprints on the Path

Upon the dusty road, my steps once bold,
Echoes linger where stories were told,
Each footprint a memory, a moment in time,
Slowly erased, like an unfinished rhyme.

The sun dips low, casting shadows so long,
The path ahead carries a haunting song,
With every step, the past gently fades,
Yet in my heart, the journey cascades.

A Stroll Through Saffron Dreams

In fields of saffron, where the sun spills gold,
I wander through visions, both tender and bold,
Each petal a whisper, each breeze a soft glow,
Painting my soul with the warmth of the flow.

The air is perfumed with sweet, fragrant sighs,
As laughter of children dances under the skies,
Embracing the colors of life in full bloom,
A tapestry woven, dispelling all gloom.

Journey's End in a Burst of Fire

As twilight descends, the horizon ignites,
A canvas of crimson, igniting the nights,
We gather the embers, our hearts all aglow,
In the warmth of the fire, our spirits will grow.

With stories to tell and dreams set ablaze,
We cherish this moment, in a fervent gaze,
For every journey concludes at the pyre,
In the whispers of night, we find our desire.

The Final Dance of Nature's Palette

In hues of crimson and gold, they fall,
The trees stand proud, yet hear their call.
A swirl of color, a fleeting grace,
Nature dons her last embrace.

With every whisper of the breeze,
They paint the ground with such ease.
Underneath the fading sun,
The dance of seasons has begun.

As twilight drapes her velvet gown,
The forest wears a fleeting crown.
A symphony of rustling leaves,
In this embrace, the heart believes.

So let us cherish the final show,
Where nature's colors softly glow.
In the fade of light, beauty found,
In this dance, we are unbound.

Quietude of the November Woods

In the silence of the fading light,
The woods breathe deep in tranquil night.
Leaves whisper tales of days gone by,
As shadows stretch and softly sigh.

Misty mornings wrap the trees,
A blanket woven by gentle breeze.
Footfalls hushed on a carpet deep,
In November's arms, the world will sleep.

Branches call to stars above,
A tranquil hymn, a song of love.
In the heart of stillness, peace descends,
The November woods, where echoes blend.

Beneath the quiet, life remains,
In whispered truths and hidden gains.
A moment held, a breath so sweet,
In nature's arms, we find our seat.

Leaves That Speak in Silence

In golden shades, they drift and sway,
Leaves like whispers, soft ballet.
They gather stories, secrets shared,
In muted tones, the heart is bared.

Each leaf a letter, cast adrift,
On autumn winds, a gentle gift.
They speak of change, of time's embrace,
In silence found, we find our place.

Rustling softly in the chill,
A symphony of nature's will.
Amongst the branches, wisdom flows,
In quietude, the spirit grows.

When footsteps fade and twilight gleams,
The leaves awaken the night's dreams.
In all they're saying, magic stirs,
In silence bound, the heart concurs.

The Dance of Dying Light

As daylight wanes and shadows creep,
The sky ignites, a promise deep.
With every hue, the world unwinds,
In the dance of light, a peace we find.

Golden rays kiss the horizon's edge,
A fleeting pact, a sacred pledge.
The heartbeat of dusk whispers low,
In dying light, the spirits glow.

Shapes elongate, the night draws near,
The crickets chirp, they sing sincere.
Nature bows in twilight's grace,
In this soft waltz, we find our place.

So let us revel in the fading sight,
Embrace the beauty of this night.
For in the dance of dying light,
A promise blooms, a new dawn's flight.

Hushed Breezes and Fading Colors

In twilight's gentle hush, the world betrays,
As leaves surrender to the cooler days.
Whispers of summer fade, soft and slow,
Painting the air with a lingering glow.

Breezes weave stories of times that have passed,
In the quietude of dusk, memories cast.
Golds and ambers swirl, a delicate dance,
As nature sighs softly, lost in a trance.

Echoes of an Evolving Season

Beneath the arch of fading skies so wide,
The earth awakens, shed layers of pride.
Emerging blooms greet the sun's tender rays,
In chorus with shadows that slowly raze.

Echoes of laughter from children at play,
Mingle with breezes that flutter and sway.
Each moment a gift, each breath in between,
A reminder of magic, of life's vibrant sheen.

The Tapestry of Rust and Gold

A tapestry woven with rust and with gold,
Presents a story, both silent and bold.
Leaves fall like secrets from branches above,
Scattering whispers of peace and of love.

Fields blush with colors no artist can seize,
Nature's own palette brings sorrow to ease.
In every rustle, a promise is told,
Of seasons revolving, of life uncontrolled.

Conversations Beneath the Canopy

Beneath the lush canopy, secrets unfold,
As branches embrace all the stories retold.
Squirrels and sparrows engage without care,
In a symphony played on the cool autumn air.

The rustling leaves join in, a soft serenade,
While shadows stretch longer, in twilight's parade.
Conversations of nature blend soft with the night,

In a world where all wonders take joyful flight.

Shadows Dancing in Thinning Light

In the fading glow of evening's embrace,
Shadows stretch long in a delicate chase.
Whispers of twilight weave through the trees,
As stars awaken from their velvet seas.

Beneath the soft hush, the world holds its breath,
Together with shadows, we dance until death.
With every flicker, the stories unfold,
As night draws its curtain, the warmth turns to cold.

When the World Turns to Ember

When the sun dips low and the skies burn bright,
The world is aglow with an ember's light.
Crimson and gold blend in a fiery embrace,
Each moment a treasure, each heartbeat a grace.

As twilight descends, the air thickens slow,
Memories smolder, like ashes they glow.
In the silence of night, dreams flicker and sway,
While embers of dusk guide us gently away.

Whispers Through the Crisp Air

In the frosty dawn, where the breath turns to mist,

Whispers float gently, too sweet to resist.
Each leaf that trembles tells tales of the past,
Of summers long gone and the moments that last.

Through the chill of the morn, secrets softly unfold,
As frost-kissed branches wear crowns of pure gold.
In the crispness of day, life begins to renew,
While echoes of glory whisper softly to you.

Maple Leaves' Silent Farewell

In the autumn's embrace, the maples take flight,
Their crimson and gold dancing, a wondrous sight.
Each leaf a soft farewell, a story to tell,
As they twirl through the air, like music from a shell.

They flutter and sway, in the cool evening breeze,

Carried by whispers that rustle the trees.
With every descent, a promise held tight,
In the cycle of seasons, they fade into night.

Glimpses of Gilded Moments

In twilight's glow, where whispers play,
The threads of gold weave night and day.
Each heartbeat echoes, soft and light,
Glimpses of joy in fading sight.

Through fragrant fields where dreams reside,
We chase the sunlight, hearts open wide.
Laughter weaves through memories spun,
A tapestry of love, forever begun.

The world a canvas, painted bright,
With strokes of hope and stars in flight.
Moments crystallized in time's embrace,
Glimpses of life, a sacred place.

When shadows stretch and day does cease,
In gilded memories, we find our peace.
With every breath, we hold on tight,
To glimpses of gold in the waning light.

The Calm Before the Embrace

In silence draped, the world awaits,
A stillness bound by time's own gates.
The waves whisper secrets to the shore,
Anticipation stirs, like never before.

Clouds gather softly, painting the sky,
As the heart beats slow, and dreams draw nigh.
Breath held heavy, like fog in the air,
The calm unfolds, with promises rare.

In this lull, where moments converge,
A feeling, profound, begins to surge.
The tension builds, sweet and sublime,
A promise of warmth in rhythm and rhyme.

With each heartbeat, love's tender trace,
Paves the pathway to that embrace.
In the hush before the vibrant bloom,
We find our way through the sultry gloom.

When Shadows Begin to Dance

As twilight descends with gentle grace,
The shadows emerge, ready to chase.
They weave their tales through trees so tall,
A whispered promise, a beckoning call.

Softly they move, in patterns divine,
A ballet of secrets, in rhythm and line.
With every flicker, the night takes her stance,
Inviting us in, when shadows begin to dance.

Stars play their parts in the velvety sky,
As echoes of laughter drift slowly by.
The moon weaves silver into night's embrace,
While shadows twirl in a timeless space.

In this fleeting moment, we breathe in the night,
Surrendering softly to the fading light.
For in each pirouette and whispering glance,
We find the magic when shadows begin to dance.

The Memory of Warmth

In the heart of winter, a flicker remains,
A soft ember glowing amid the cold rains.
It carries the echoes of laughter and cheer,
The comfort of moments we hold so dear.

Wrapped in the warmth of a gentle embrace,
Familiar faces with smiles we can't replace.
Each memory lingers like a sweet, tender song,
A refuge from storms, where we all belong.

Through frostbitten nights, when the world feels bleak,
The warmth of our shared tales is what we seek.
We gather like moths, drawn to the light,
In the memory of warmth that conquers the night.

So let us remember, as cold winds blow free,
The warmth of our hearts, our shared history.
For in every heartbeat and every fond glance,
Lies the memory of warmth, a continuing dance.

The Chill of Seasonal Change

As summer's warmth begins to wane,
A whisper of frost dances in the air,
Leaves turn gold, then brown with disdain,
Nature prepares for a winter's snare.

Days grow short, the sun sinks low,
A gentle reminder of time's swift flight,
The trees stand bare, no longer aglow,
Embracing the silence of the coming night.

Melodies of Withering Petals

Beneath the arch of ancient trees,
Petals flutter, one last farewell,
Their dance like soft whispers in the breeze,
A canvas of memories they gently swell.

With colors that fade, their beauty remains,
A symphony sweet, though life must depart,
In the heart of decay, the sweetest refrains,
Melodies linger, painted in art.

Canvas of September Skies

September paints the heavens bright,
Brushstrokes of orange and dusky gray,
Clouds drift like thoughts on the cusp of night,
As twilight settles, bids farewell to day.

The sun dips low, its warmth still clings,
While stars awaken from their slumber deep,
Each moment crafted, like a song that sings,
In the vast expanse where dreams softly creep.

The Poetry of Decaying Splendor

In the heart of autumn, beauty wanes,
Splendor found in the rust of decay,
Nature's canvas bears rich, bittersweet stains,
As echoes of life slowly drift away.

Yet in every crumbling leaf, there's a tale,
Of moments that flourished, then fell to the ground,
There's grace in their fall, a whisper, a wail,
The poetry of life and death intertwined.

The Language of Falling Leaves

Whispers in the quiet woods, they fall,
A symphony of colors, red and gold,
In every flutter is a tale to tell,
Of summer's laughter, now grown old.

They dance like flames, in crisp, cool air,
Spinning down from branches high,
With every drop, a secret shared,
In the gentle hush, they sigh.

Nature's parchment, written in hues,
A legacy of time, softly conveyed,
Each leaf, a memory, forever imbues,
In the heart of the earth, their stories laid.

As twilight falls and shadows blend,
They whisper dreams of seasons past,
In their silent language, we comprehend,
Life's fleeting moments, too precious to last.

Stories Carried by November's Breath

In the chill of November's breath,
Leaves rustle secrets, half-heard and near,
Each gust unveils a tale of death,
Yet hints at life when skies are clear.

The trees stand tall, their silhouettes stark,
Against a canvas of gray and gloom,
But in the whispers, there's a spark,
Of warmth awaiting when flowers bloom.

Underneath the weight of twilight's veil,
Ghosts of autumn linger, bittersweet,
In every sigh and every wail,
Lies the promise of new life, discreet.

So let the winds carry forth the lore,
Of storms that passed and skies that shined,
With every breath, we yearn for more,
In November's tale, hope intertwined.

Gossamer Threads of Silver Light

In the hush of dawn, where dreams alight,
Gossamer threads weave tales so bright,
Each ray a whisper, soft and slight,
Kissing the world in the morning's sight.

Through dewdrops glistening on the grass,
They dance in patterns, a fleeting ballet,
A tapestry spun from moments that pass,
Illuminating paths where shadows play.

With each flutter of the dove's soft wing,
In the tangled web where memories cling,
Silver light beckons, an ancient spring,
Lifting the heart, making the spirit sing.

In this delicate dawn, as hours unfold,
Gossamer threads, tender and bold,
We find our stories, in whispers retold,
In the light of the morning, our dreams are gold.

Memories Wrapped in Frosted Air

In the stillness of winter's embrace,
Frost-kissed mornings, serene and bare,
Every breath forms a delicate trace,
As memories linger in frigid air.

Time stands frozen in this quiet realm,
Where echoes of laughter softly arise,
Wrapped in blankets of white, at the helm,
Of secrets held under gray, clouded skies.

Each crystal flake, a story enshrined,
Carved from the moments that once flew by,
Reminders of warmth, of love intertwined,
In the chill of the day, beneath the vast sky.

So let us wander, hand in hand,
Through the fields of glitter, where silence sings,
In memories wrapped, we make our stand,
Finding solace in the beauty winter brings.

The Last Flicker of Daylight

As twilight descends on the weary hills,
The sun dips low, painting shadows and thrills.
With hues of amber and whispers of night,
The world holds its breath in the fading light.

Stars begin to twinkle in the darkening dome,
While crickets pipe their songs, calling us home.
In this gentle moment, where dreams intertwine,
The last flicker of daylight feels sacred, divine.

Whispering Fields of Solitude

In fields where the tall grasses dance with the breeze,
Silence speaks louder than all worldly pleas.
Each rustle, a secret, each shadow, a song,
In solitude's cradle, we quietly belong.

The horizon extends, a canvas untamed,
With echoes of laughter from memories unnamed.

Here, time bends slowly under nature's embrace,
In whispering fields, we find our own space.

Beneath the Veil of Maturing Skies

Under a tapestry of clouds brushed with gray,
Life subtly shifts in the waning of day.
Sunbeams like fingers reach out and explore,
While the heavens, in layers, tell tales of yore.

In quiet introspection, the soul finds its voice,
Each cloud, a reminder to ponder and rejoice.
With storms on the horizon, and calmness in sight,
Beneath the veil of maturing skies, we take flight.

The Transition of the Heart

With every heartbeat, a story unfolds,
A journey through shadows, of warmth and of cold.
In moments of joy and in struggles we face,
The transition of heart weaves a delicate lace.

It dances in rhythm, a waltz of the free,
From fragile whispers to bold symphony.
As petals unfurl in the soft morning glow,
The heart's transition teaches us how to grow.

Veils of Amber and Olive

Beneath the trees where shadows play,
Veils of amber gently sway,
Olive branches intertwine,
Nature whispers, hearts align.

Golden hues kiss the breeze,
Timeless secrets in the leaves,
In this grove, our spirits blend,
In the light, we find our end.

Echoes of laughter fill the air,
A tapestry woven with love and care,
Tender moments, forever caught,
In veils of amber, dreams are sought.

Together we wander, hand in hand,
Through this enchanted, whispered land,
In every rustle, a story told,
Of love cherished and never old.

In the Grip of Vintage Yesterdays

Faded photographs in dusty frames,
Memories linger, calling names,
In sepia tones, we find our past,
Moments captured, meant to last.

Old records spin on a weathered turn,
From smoky bars, sweet lessons learned,
Each note a journey down the lane,
In the grip of nostalgia's chain.

Worn-out letters, inked with care,
Whispers of love, secrets laid bare,
Every heartbeat, echoing through time,
In vintage days, our souls entwine.

As sunlight wanes on the day,
We embrace the shadows, come what may,
For in the past, our stories play,
Forever held in vintage yesterdays.

A Whispered Farewell to Sunlight

As twilight descends, the world slows down,
A whispered farewell to the day's golden crown,
Shadows stretch long, and colors fade,
In this quiet moment, beauty is made.

The last rays dance on the crest of the hill,
A gentle sigh, the heart stays still,
In the silence, a soft goodbye,
To the warmth that bids us fly.

Stars awaken, one by one,
Covering the canvas where day was spun,
In the embrace of the cool night air,
We honor the light, with whispers and prayer.

So let the darkness cradle your dreams,
For the moonlight will drape us in silvery beams,
And though the sunset bids us depart,
Its warmth lingers on in our hearts.

Where Memories Dance with the Leaves

In the autumn grove where silence sings,
Leaves twirl down on whispered wings,
Every rustle tells a tale untold,
Where memories dance, in colors bold.

Crimson and gold, a vibrant swirl,
Beneath the branches, the past unfurls,
With each footfall, echoes collide,
In the embrace of the trees, we can hide.

Moments captured in the fading light,
Laughter woven with pure delight,
In this sanctuary, lost in time,
Every heartbeat, a subtle rhyme.

So let us gather, hand in hand,
Where the leaves drift softly to the land,
For in this dance, we are set free,
Where memories swirl, eternally.

A Serenade for Swaying Trees

In whispered tones, the branches sway,
Their leafy laughter fills the day.
Dancing shadows on the ground,
Nature's symphony, a gentle sound.

Beneath the sky, the breezes roam,
Each rustle sings of ages home.
Roots deep in earth, they know the tale,
Of sunlit dawns and moonlit sail.

With every gust, a secret shared,
In leafy arms, the world repaired.
They bend and bow, with grace they lead,
Their tender hearts, the breath of trees.

The Golden Hour's Confession

As sunlight spills in amber hues,
The day reveals its hidden views.
Soft whispers wrap the world in light,
Embracing shadows, chasing night.

The horizon blushes, secrets told,
Time's gentle brush, a sight to behold.
Each ray a promise, fleeting, bright,
A confessional kiss from day to night.

With every minute, colors blend,
A masterpiece that cannot end.
In twilight's grasp, our hearts take flight,
The golden hour, our shared delight.

Serenity in Nature's Decline

Amidst the rust and fading grace,
The whispers of time leave their trace.
Leaves turn to gold, the branches bare,
In nature's end, a quiet prayer.

A soft decay, a tender sigh,
Where once was laughter, now goodbye.
Yet in the stillness, beauty gleams,
In every ending, hope redeems.

The sun sets low, painting the sky,
In hues of sorrow, spirits fly.
Every withered petal tells its tale,
Of lives once vibrant, now grown pale.

Reflections on Crimson Waters

Beneath the sky of molten gold,
The waters dance, their stories told.
A crimson hue, a gentle flow,
Mirroring dreams that ebb and glow.

Each ripple carries whispers faint,
Of memories lost, and those that ain't.
In twilight's grasp, the world stands still,
As silence weaves a magic thrill.

The trees lean low, in hush they stare,
At liquid glass, their hearts laid bare.
In every splash, a heartbeat's spark,
Reflections linger, love in the dark.

Sonnet of the Falling Dusk

As twilight whispers secrets to the day,
The sky adorned in hues of soft despair,
A gentle breeze begins its tender play,
While shadows stretch and reach to find a pair.

The stars awaken, shyly peeking through,
Each one a dream that dances in the night,
In twilight's embrace, the world seems anew,
A canvas painted with a lover's light.

With every heartbeat, time begins to slow,
The dusk unfolds like petals in the breeze,
A silent promise only few may know,
Where whispers linger, carried by the leaves.

The Approach of an Orange Horizon

Beneath the vault of heaven burning bright,
An orange blaze ignites the waking sky,
With every shade, the dawn begins its flight,
As dreams dissolve and daylight dares to pry.

The clouds, like brushstrokes, soften in the glow,
A canvas stretching far beyond the eye,
Each vibrant hue a tale that they bestow,
A fleeting moment that we cannot buy.

And though the day will chase the night away,
This fleeting dance of colors won't forget,
For in the heart, the sunset seems to stay,
A memory wrapped in warm hues, set.

Rustling Secrets of the Forest

In verdant hush, where sunlight weaves its thread,

The trees stand tall, their wisdom clad in green,
Through rustling leaves, the whispers softly spread,
A symphony where nature's heart is seen.

Each step unveils the stories intertwined,
With roots in soil, deep knowledge they possess,
In every shadow, secrets left behind,
An ancient power wrapped in vastness' dress.

The mossy floor, a tapestry of life,
Each creature adds to tales of olden days,
The forest breathes, a world without strife,
Where silence speaks in gentle, woven ways.

Yearning in a Dwindling Day

As daylight wanes, the shadows start to blend,
The golden rays slip slowly from their grace,
With every breath, I find a heart to mend,
Longing for moments time cannot erase.

The clock ticks softly, marking down the time,
Yet every glance retains a cherished spark,
In fading light, I hear the distant chime,
Of memories that linger in the dark.

Oh, let me hold this twilight in my heart,
A bridge to dreams that linger just outside,
For every ending helps a new day start,
In every dusk, the hope cannot be denied.

The Melody of Falling Rain

A symphony of whispers in the night,
Soft drumming on the window, pure delight,
Each drop a note, a gentle serenade,
Nature's song, in silver hues displayed.

Puddles form like mirrors on the ground,
Reflecting dreams where silent hopes abound,
As clouds drift slowly, painting skies anew,
The world awash in every shade of blue.

With every splash, the earth begins to breathe,
Awakening the blooms that brightly seethe,
In rhythm with the storm, life starts again,
A waltz of hearts beneath the falling rain.

Embracing every raindrop's cool caress,
The melody unfolds, no need to confess,
In nature's arms, we find our solace there,
A fleeting moment, hanging in the air.

Savoring the Breath of Change

As summer wanes, the leaves begin to fold,
Transforming hues, their stories softly told,
Upon the breeze, a scent of dusk arrives,
Reminding hearts that every moment thrives.

With each new dawn, the world sheds its skin,
Embracing cycles, letting warmth begin,
The fragile bond of past held in the light,
Savoring the breath of change, so bright.

In whispered winds, the secrets of the trees,
As seasons dance, they sway with grace and ease,

Ripe fruits adorn the branches, sweet and free,
A taste of life, unfolding endlessly.

So let us linger in this fleeting hour,
As colors blend, and blossoms whisper power,
For every shift unveils a new embrace,
In savoring the breath of change, we trace.

Reflections of a Wandering Mind

In quiet corners of the heart we roam,
Exploring thoughts that lead us far from home,
Each idea, a spark, a flickering flame,
Casting shadows, yet never quite the same.

The tapestry of dreams begins to weave,
Threads of wonder, moments we believe,
Wandering pathways made of hopes and fears,
Glistening like dewdrops, mingling with tears.

As dusk descends, the stars appear in streams,
Echoes of laughter fold into our dreams,
Reflecting visions of what could have been,
In the dark's embrace, the light seeps in.

So let the currents of thought take their flight,
For in the wander, we find our own light,
Reflections of a mind, forever free,
A journey crafted through our reverie.

The Final Flourish of Flora

As autumn whispers to the fading bloom,
A tapestry of colors starts to loom,
With every petal falling to the ground,
The final flourish of flora, profound.

Once vibrant greens now crinkle, drift, and sway,

As days grow short and gentle shadows play,
A symphony of crispness fills the air,
In golden light, the world begins to care.

Yet through the stillness, life's essence persists,
In every seed, a promise still exists,
A waiting hush for what is yet to come,
In quietude, the echoes make us numb.

So let the petals fall, a soft goodbye,
Each ending bears the spark of the nearby,
For in the cycle, nature finds her way,
A final flourish, rekindling the day.

Garland of Brown and Burgundy

In autumn's grasp, the leaves do fall,
A carpet rich, brown whispers call,
Burgundy hues in twilight gleam,
Nature weaves her fading dream.

Branches sway, a gentle tune,
As dusk descends beneath the moon,
Rustling tales of seasons past,
In every shadow, memories cast.

A garland woven, soft and warm,
Holding close the weathered charm,
Time's embrace around each hue,
A tapestry of life anew.

Beneath the sky so grand and wide,
We stroll where all our dreams reside,
In brown and burgundy, sweetly spun,
Eternal dance, two hearts as one.

Lessons from a Fading Sun

The sun dips low, a golden sigh,
Whispers secrets as daylight dies,
In twilight's grasp, the shadows stretch,
A canvas rich, the heartache etched.

Each fading ray, a time doth teach,
That solace lies within the breach,
As colors blend, both bold and meek,
Life finds the strength in what is weak.

From warmth to dusk, we learn to yield,
Embrace the night, the truths concealed,
For every end, a spark will rise,
Lessons bright beneath the skies.

In silence, wisdom takes its flight,
The beauty found in darkest night,
So let the sun set on the day,
And trust the dawn will find a way.

The Harvest of Heartfelt Memories

In fields of gold, where laughter grew,
Moments cherished, hearts so true,
We gather close, the ties that bind,
A harvest rich, love intertwined.

With every grain, a story's spun,
Of summer's warmth and winter's run,
These woven threads, a tapestry,
Each memory sings a symphony.

We walk the rows, both old and new,
Recalling dreams that once we knew,
Fruits of kindness, warmth, and grace,
Found in each familiar face.

So let the seasons come and go,
We'll plant our seeds, watch tendrils grow,
For in this land of heartfelt cheer,
The harvest blooms each passing year.

Fables of the Forest Floor

Beneath the boughs, in shadows deep,
Where secrets in the silence sleep,
The forest whispers fables old,
In every rustle, stories told.

The mossy ground, a tapestry,
Of life and death, of mystery,
Each step unveils a hidden song,
Where creatures hum the tales of long.

In burrows soft, the mischief stirs,
While owls spin tales of twilight blurs,
A symphony of sound and breath,
Life dances close to nature's depth.

So listen well to nature's lore,
For wisdom dwells on the forest floor,
In harmony, we find our place,
Amongst the fables, boundless grace.

Leaves in the Gentle Breeze

In the hush of autumn's sigh,
Leaves dance lightly, spirits high,
Whispers carried on the air,
Nature's song beyond compare.

Crimson, amber, flutter down,
Painting earth with nature's crown,
In each twist, a tale unfolds,
Of summer's warmth and winter's cold.

Beneath the boughs, a carpet lies,
A tapestry where beauty thrives,
Children laugh, and dreams take flight,
In the embrace of day's soft light.

As twilight casts its golden hue,
The breeze reminds of joys anew,
With every leaf that finds its place,
The world transforms, a sacred space.

Echoes of Harvest's Breath

In fields of plenty, golden hue,
The earth awakens, fresh and true,
Harvest whispers through the grain,
Promises of joy through patience' strain.

Cornstalks swaying in the sun,
Gathering stories, one by one,
Beneath the weight of ripened dreams,
Echoes flow like silver streams.

The farmer's hands, a map of toil,
Reaping blessings from the soil,
With every turn, a blessing shared,
With whispered thanks, the heart laid bare.

As twilight falls and shadows creep,
A bounty gathered, rich and deep,
In the twilight's soft caress,
The echoes sing of nature's bless.

A Symphony of Falling Gold

Notes of amber fill the sky,
As trees release their children high,
A symphony of rustling sound,
Where nature's rhythms can be found.

Each golden leaf, a whispered prayer,
Spinning gently through crisp air,
The wind conducts this timeless score,
As nature plays forevermore.

Together swaying, a gentle sway,
In autumn's breath, they dance and play,
The world transformed in golden light,
As day departs into the night.

So let us join this fleeting dance,
In laughter, joy, and sweet romance,
For every moment we hold tight,
Is music woven into the night.

Secrets of the Waving Branches

In the cradle of the towering trees,
Whispers ride on the playful breeze,
Secrets tangled in the leaves,
Stories etched in the bark that weaves.

Branches stretching, reaching wide,
Beneath their shade, our dreams can hide,
In the quiet, what tales they tell,
Of suns that rise and those that fell.

The rustle hints of laughter past,
Of lovers found and friendships cast,
In the dance of twilight shadows,
Life spins on where the river flows.

So pause awhile beneath their gaze,
And let your heart begin to blaze,
For in their sway, we come to see,
The secrets held in nature's glee.

Echoes of Ailing Aspects

In shadows cast by crumbling walls,
Where whispers of the past still call,
The echoes linger, soft yet stark,
A haunting hymn in silence dark.

Each step we take on hollow ground,
Reveals the stories long unwound,
In fading light, the truth unfolds,
Of dreams once bright, now turned to gold.

Yet in the aching, there's a grace,
A fragile thread in time's embrace,
For every wound, a seed is sown,
In sorrow's depth, new strength is grown.

So let us listen, hearts attuned,
To lessons from the past that crooned,
For in the echoes, we shall find,
The strength to leave the dark behind.

An Elegy for Enchanted Woods

Beneath the boughs where fairies danced,
A tapestry of dreams enhanced,
The leaves now whisper tales of woe,
In the stillness where the wild things go.

The trunks stand bare, their stories old,
In rings of time, their secrets hold,
Yet through the shadows, light will pierce,
A remembrance sweet as nature's verse.

The breeze recalls the laughter shared,
With every branch and root ensnared,
Yet even in this mournful shroud,
Life stirs beneath the heavy cloud.

So mourn we must, yet celebrate,
The magic that weaves through fate,
For in our hearts, the woods will thrive,
In every breath, the past survives.

Harvesting Dreams from Frosted Air

In dawn's soft blush, where whispers freeze,
A tapestry of dreams takes ease,
Each breath a cloud, each heartbeat's song,
In winter's hold, where spirits long.

Beneath the frost, the seeds lie stirred,
While echoes of the past are heard,
Each glimmered hope a fleeting gain,
In nature's silence, wisdom reigns.

The fields are still, yet promise grows,
In shimmering veils of frost that froze,
With every thaw, new life appears,
Harvesting dreams from shadowed years.

So hold the light, though days be cold,
For in each moment, stories told,
A warmth shall rise, a fire ignite,
In frosted air, our dreams take flight.

The Savoring of Subtle Change

In gentle sighs, the seasons blend,
A melody that will not end,
With every leaf that sways and twirls,
Life's tapestry unfurls and swirls.

The dawn is painted soft and new,
While shadows cast in evening hue,
Each moment whispers, sweet and strange,
In quiet grace, we sense the change.

The bud breaks forth, the bloom will fade,
Yet in this dance, no step betrayed,
For time is but a fleeting song,
In every chord, we all belong.

So let us taste each subtle shift,
Embrace the flow, our spirits lift,
For in each change, a gift is found,
A savoring of life renowned.

Embrace of the Gathering Shadows

In twilight's arms, the whispers play,
Secrets fold as night greets day,
Silhouettes dance in a soft, dark hue,
The world beneath finds peace anew.

Shadows stretch with a gentle grace,
Embracing dreams in that sacred space,
A lullaby of dusk softly calls,
Where stillness reigns and nightfall stalls.

Stars awaken, twinkling bright,
Painting the canvas of the night,
As twilight drapes a velvet shroud,
The heart finds comfort among the crowd.

In every corner where shadows creep,
Lies an embrace that cradles the deep,
A refuge found in the cool embrace,
Of gathering shadows, we find our place.

The Stillness Before the Snow

The air is hushed, a breath held tight,
As nature waits for the fall of white,
Branches bare in the twilight glow,
In the stillness that precedes the snow.

Time pauses gently, like a sigh,
Clouds gather round the darkening sky,
A promise lingers with every breeze,
In the quiet before the world's freeze.

Footsteps are softened, echoes of peace,
As hearts lean in for a brief release,
Dreams wrapped warm in a snowy shroud,
In the stillness, the earth feels proud.

Moments hang like crystals aglow,
Awaiting the kiss of the soft, white snow,
Nature whispers in anticipation sweet,
The stillness before holds joy complete.

Hues of Sorrow and Solace

In the twilight hues, the heart does ache,
Fragments of joy, the soul does take,
Shadows of sorrow paint the day,
Yet find their solace in twilight's play.

Beneath the gray, a palette unfolds,
Stories of warmth that the sun once told,
Colors bleed in a gentle embrace,
As the heart recalls its rightful place.

Through the tears, gold still shines bright,
A tapestry woven in the soft twilight,
For every sorrow holds a trace,
Of calm and comfort in memory's grace.

In the dance of hues, the spirit finds,
Harmony where the heart unwinds,
A vibrant spectrum, both deep and vast,
In hues of sorrow, solace is cast.

The Sigh of Nature's Retreat

When autumn whispers its soft goodbye,
Leaves descend like a gentle sigh,
Nature folds into a quiet rest,
In the cradle of earth, the heart feels blessed.

Fields that shimmer with a golden hue,
Abandon their dance, bid adieu,
Branches stand bare against the sky,
In the pause of nature, the soul learns to fly.

Clouds drift lazily, as if to say,
All things must yield to the end of day,
A breath is taken, a moment spans,
In the sigh of retreat, life takes its stance.

Winter waits with an open heart,
To paint the world with its purest art,
And in the silence, the spirit renews,
In nature's retreat, the essence ensues.

In the Arms of Dwindling Light

In twilight's hush, where shadows weave,
The day concedes, and night takes leave.
Soft whispers brush the weary trees,
As fading sun dips beneath the breeze.

Gentle hues of orange sigh,
Paint the clouds in a slow goodbye.
The stars awaken, one by one,
In the embrace of a setting sun.

Memories linger in the amber glow,
Where time stands still, and dreams can flow.
A final dance of radiant rays,
Cradled softly in evening's embrace.

With each heartbeat, the world unwinds,
In the arms of dusk, solace we find.
The light may fade, but hearts will ignite,
In the beauty born of dwindling light.

The Echo of Yesterday's Blooms

In gardens past, where colors played,
The petals whispered in soft cascade.
Each bloom a jewel, each scent a song,
With memories tracing where they belong.

The laughter dances on the breeze,
As sunlight trickles through ancient trees.
Echoes of summer, a fragrant embrace,
Awakening warmth in nature's grace.

Yet time unfolds, as seasons do,
Fading the splendor, painting anew.
But in the heart, their essence remains,
The echoes of blooms in endless refrains.

So let the petals fall where they may,
For yesterday's blooms still brighten the day.
In memories kept, so vividly drawn,
The echoes of yesterday's blooms live on.

Colors of Remembrance

In the palette of time, colors collide,
Shades of laughter, where sorrows reside.
A canvas of moments, both joyful and wild,
Each hue tells a story, a heart of a child.

Golden sunrises paint hopes that ignite,
While sapphire twilight brings peace to the night.

The emerald whispers of trees hold the past,
In hues of nostalgia, forever to last.

Crimson of courage, with trials and strife,
Blending with shadows that shimmer with life.
As the brushstrokes of memory start to unfurl,
The colors of remembrance dance and swirl.

For every feeling, a shade finds its place,
In the tapestry woven with love and grace.
In the heart's gallery, forever they stay,
The colors of remembrance, brightening our way.

The Last Song of the Crickets

In the quiet dusk, where shadows play,
The crickets chirp, bidding farewell to day.
A symphony woven in the depths of night,
Their final song, a gentle delight.

With haunting notes, they serenade the stars,
A chorus of dreams, like distant guitars.
Each trill a memory, a moment reprieved,
In melodies woven, all sorrow retrieved.

As moonlight drapes on the soft, dewy grass,
They sing of the hours that quickly did pass.
In the tapestry of air, their voices entwined,
The last song of crickets, a treasure defined.

So listen closely as day bids goodbye,
For in their soft lullabies, echoes always lie.
A reminder of moments, now whispered in air,
Of the last song of the crickets, a musical prayer.

Secret Notes on the Breeze

Whispers dance through tangled trees,
A melody carried on the gentle sighs,
Each leaf a secret, each gust a tease,
Nature's whispers, where our heart lies.

Promises float like feathers in flight,
In the quiet of twilight, they softly gleam,
The story of love under stars so bright,
In the silence, we find our dream.

Echoes of laughter in the evening air,
The rustle tells tales of moments we shared,
Floating on breezes, free from all care,
In every soft sigh, our spirits are bared.

A symphony played on the strings of the night,
With every note, our lives intertwine,
In each breath, the world feels just right,
Secret notes on the breeze, forever divine.

The Solace of Slowly Fading

In the waning glow of a sun-kissed day,
Colors dissolve like dreams in the night,
A gentle retreat, as shadows hold sway,
The world whispers softly, surrendering light.

With each passing breath, the twilight draws near,

Echoes of laughter drift tender and low,
Embraced by the quiet, we conquer our fear,
In the fading embrace of the soft afterglow.

Time hums a lullaby, soothing and sweet,
The day's troubled worries, now softened, they yield,
In the stillness, our hearts find their beat,
In quiet surrender, the night is our shield.

So let us linger, let moments unwind,
In the solace of fading, we find what we seek,
In the dimming of day, our souls are aligned,
In the beauty of dusk, we gather our peace.

Glimmers of Glistening Mornings

Awakening softly, the dawn paints the sky,
With hues that shimmer and dance on the dew,
Each ray a promise, a fresh lullaby,
In glimmers of hope, the world feels anew.

Birds serenade, their sweet songs take flight,
Breaking the silence with joyous refrain,
Nature's revival, a magnificent sight,
Each glimmer a treasure, where dreams can sustain.

The whispering winds gently cradle the trees,
As sunbeams weave stories that twinkle and play,

In this symphony of life, our hearts find their keys,
Unlocking the wonders that greet us each day.

So let us embrace this glistening morn,
With open hearts and spirits that soar,
In each fleeting moment, a new life is born,
In glimmers of mornings, we cherish and explore.

The Sound of Dust Settling

In the corners of rooms where memories dwell,
The sound of dust settling speaks of the past,
Whispers of stories, only time can tell,
In silence profound, every moment locked fast.

Each grain carries echoes of laughter and tears,
Of love that was forged, and dreams that took flight,
In the stillness, we honor those yesteryear fears,
The soft sigh of history, cloaked in the night.

As shadows now linger and sunlight drifts low,
A tapestry woven of days gone before,
The dust dances lightly, a delicate show,
A reminder that life is a journey, not lore.

So let it settle, this dust of our days,
In the quiet of now, we breathe and we feel,
For in every whisper, life's intricate ways,
The sound of dust settling, our truth is revealed.

www.ingramcontent.com/pod-product-compliance
Lightning Source LLC
LaVergne TN
LVHW010552070526
838199LV00063BA/4954